J599.884 B432
Bender, Lionel.
Gorillas

WITHDRAWN
FROM THE RECORDS OF THE
MID-CONTINENT PUBLIC LIBRARY

MID-CONTINENT PUBLIC LIBRARY
Blue Springs North Branch
850 N. Hunter Drive
Blue Springs, MO 64015

BN

D1362128

Wild Animals

GORILLA

Lionel Bender

Chrysalis Education

This U.S. edition copyright © 2005 Chrysalis Education
Published in conjunction with Chrysalis Books Group PLC
International copyright reserved in all countries.
No part of this book may be reproduced in any
form without written permission from the publisher.

Distributed in the United States by
Smart Apple Media
2140 Howard Drive West
North Mankato, Minnesota 56003

Library of Congress Control Number: 2004108639

ISBN 1-59389-190-3

Editorial Manager: Joyce Bentley
Senior Editor: Rasha Elsaeed
Editorial Assistant: Camilla Lloyd

Produced by Bender Richardson White, U.K.
Project Editor: Lionel Bender
Designer: Ben White
Production: Kim Richardson
Picture Researcher: Cathy Stastny
Cover Make-up: Mike Pilley, Radius

Printed in China

10 9 8 7 6 5 4 3 2 1

MID-CONTINENT PUBLIC LIBRARY - BTM

3 0003 00070238 9

MID-CONTINENT PUBLIC LIBRARY
Blue Springs North Branch
850 N. Hunter Drive
Blue Springs, MO 64015
BN

Words in **bold** can be found in New words on page 31.

Picture credits
Cover : © Digital Vision.
© Digital Vision: pages 1, 2, 4, 9, 10, 12, 13, 16, 17, 18, 19, 21, 23, 24, 25. © Corbis Images Inc.: pages
17 (Paul A. Sauders), 24 (Rob C. Nunnington/Gallo Images), 27 (Kevin Schafer/Corbis,
29 (Reuters/Corbis Images). © Frank Lane Picture Agency Limited: pages 5 (Mark Newman),
6 (E. & O. Hosking), 8 (Phil Ward), 14 (Frank Lanting/Minden Pictures), 15 (Silvestris Fotoservice),
20 (Silvestris Fotoservice), 22 (Silvestris Fotoservice), 26 (C. Ellis/Minden Pictures), 28 (Silvestris
Fotoservice), 29 (P. Ward). © RSPCA Photolibrary: pages 7 (Andrew Routh), 11 (Alyson Pearce).

Contents

Big gorillas

Gorillas are much like humans and chimpanzees but bigger.

They can grow 6 ft 4 in (1.9 m) tall and weigh 200 kg (440 lb). A gorilla can live for 30 years.

Homes

Gorillas live in **rainforests** in the middle of Africa.

Some gorillas live on **lowlands**, where it is warm. Others live in cool areas in the mountains.

Food

The gorilla eats mostly plants.
Its favorite foods are leaves
and stems.

A gorilla also eat fruits, ferns, and nettles. If it is very hungry, it will eat snails and slugs.

Among the trees

A gorilla walks 1000 yards (1 km) a day to find food. It spends most of its time resting and eating.

Each evening, a gorilla makes a **nest** in the trees. Here it sleeps.

Living together

Gorillas live in groups. The biggest male is the leader in each group.

An **adult** male gorilla is bigger and stronger than an adult female. It also has more hair.

Senses

The gorilla has good hearing, eyesight, and **sense** of smell.

It touches things and picks them up with its hands.

Defenses

An adult gorilla is so big that few animals dare to threaten it.

Male gorillas have four big, pointed teeth. They use them in fights and to scare off enemies.

Skin and fur

The gorilla has tough skin. The skin is covered in **fur**.

Gorillas clean each other's fur. They pick out dirt and insects with their fingers.

Family life

A mother gorilla has one baby at a time. She feeds it on her milk until it is eight months old.

The baby is looked after by
older gorillas in its family.

Growing up

The young gorilla learns to feed, make nests, and climb trees.

Young gorillas stay close to their mothers until they are two years old.

Becoming an adult

Male gorillas are adult at age 15. Females are adult at age seven or eight years.

Young adult males leave their groups and live alone. Later they are joined by adult females.

In danger

Farmers are cutting down forests to make fields. They are destroying the gorillas' home.

Some people kill gorillas for their meat or for their **skulls** or skins, which are sold as gifts.

Gorilla care

Scientists study gorillas in the wild to find out how to help the animals survive.

Young gorillas are looked after and their homes made into safe wildlife areas.

Quiz

1 How big do gorillas grow?

2 Where do gorillas live?

3 What do gorillas eat?

4 Where do gorillas sleep at night?

5 How long does a mother gorilla feed
her baby with her milk?

6 At what age do young gorillas start to go off
on their own?

7 Which are bigger—adult male or adult female gorillas?

8 Why do some people kill gorillas?

The answers are all in this book!

New words

adult fully grown and able to make babies.

fur thick hair that covers most of the body.

lowlands large area of generally flat land surrounding hills and mountains.

nest sort of bed or home made by an animal.

rainforests areas of trees that get lots of rain all year round. Most rainforests are in the middle of South America, Africa, and Southeast Asia.

sense the way animals find out about their surroundings. Animals have five senses—sight, hearing, smell, taste, and touch. The body senses something when it notices it is there.

skull skeleton, or bony structure, of the head.

Index

X075331

This Little Tiger book
belongs to:

_____

_____

_____

KU-632-958

For Elliot xx

LITTLE TIGER PRESS LTD,
an imprint of the Little Tiger Group
1 Coda Studios, 189 Munster Road, London SW6 6AW
www.littletiger.co.uk

First published in Great Britain 2019
This edition published 2020

Text and illustrations by Joanne Partis
Text and illustrations copyright © Little Tiger Press 2019

A CIP catalogue record for this book is available from
the British Library

All rights reserved • ISBN 978-1-78881-716-5

Printed in China • LTP/1400/1335/0320

2 4 6 8 10 9 7 5 3 1

Oh NO, BEAR!

JOANNE PARTIS

LITTLE TIGER

LONDON

Hello, Bear!
Bear has woken up
and he is HUNGRY!

"I have an important thing to do today," thinks Bear.

"Now, what is it . . . ?"

Bear's list of things to do today.
1. Eat
2. Sleep

A lovely smell is drifting through the forest.
It is **very** distracting!

Sniff . . .

Sniff . . .

Bear has a clever nose. It is very good at following delicious smells.

And delicious smells like this can mean only one thing.
FOOD!

"Hello, Bear!" It's Rabbit and her friends.
They're very busy digging up carrots.

What an **enormous** pile!
  "Try a carrot!" offers Rabbit.
  "Well, if you insist," says Bear.

"This one is good," thinks Bear, having a nibble. "And this one is particularly . . .

. . . CARROTY.

And I'll just have a little try of this one . . ."

OH NO, BEAR!

Oh dear.

The wheelbarrow of carrots
seems to be empty.

"Where are our carrots?" asks Rabbit.
"We spent ages picking them!"

"I'm sorry," mumbles Bear. "I only meant to have
a little taste."

Bear looks at the field of carrots waiting to
be picked. But before he can think of a very
helpful idea, his nose begins to tingle.

Another lovely smell is drifting past.

Bear forgets all about helping poor Rabbit
and sets off after it.

Careful where you're treading, Bear!

"Hello, Bear!" says Squirrel. She's been very busy picking delicious acorns with her friends.

To a bear with a hungry tummy and a clever nose,
acorns smell fantastic!

"Would you like to help us pick some?" asks Squirrel.
"You can try some, too!"

"Yes please!" says Bear eagerly. "Mmmm," he munches
happily. It is hard to say much with a large mouthful
of tasty acorns.

"Mmmmm,

MMMmm,

MMMMM!"

OH NO, BEAR!

Oh dear. It's happened again.

"You were supposed to fill up the baskets, not your tummy!" grumbles Squirrel.

It is amazing quite how many acorns will fit in a hungry bear's tummy.

"I'm sorry," says Bear. "Maybe I could help you find some more acorn trees?" Bear looks around but . . .

Sniff . . .

It's very hard to concentrate when . . .

Sniff . . .

Yet another tempting smell comes drifting through the trees.

"SLOW
DOWN,
BEAR!"

"Hello, Bear,"
waves Beaver. "Look at the
lovely fish I've caught for
my tea."

"I won't eat Beaver's fish," Bear thinks to himself.
He is sure that he can resist this time.

"Have a little taste if you like!" shouts Beaver.

Oh dear.

Bear has accidentally eaten Beaver's fish.

"That was supposed to be my tea!" moans Beaver.

"I was trying so hard not to eat it," says Bear sadly. "I wonder if maybe there are more fish in the river?"

Bear jumps in . . .

SPLASH!

"No," he splutters. "None in here."

Bear can't find any fish at all. Where have they all gone?

"I'm sorry, Beaver," says Bear gloomily. "I ate the only fish in the whole river."

Time to be off, Bear thinks.

Poor Bear. Things really haven't gone right today at all.

"I shouldn't have eaten Beaver's fish," says Bear to himself, rubbing his rather large belly.

"Or Squirrel's acorns.

OR Rabbit's carrots."

What if Bear's friends are angry with him? And what if they go hungry all winter?

"I will go straight back to my cave to do some extra hard thinking," yawns Bear, suddenly feeling very sleepy.

"I will think up a way to make all my friends happy again."

But when he gets home, Bear can't squeeze
his tummy through the front door.
Bear is very confused.

He's **sure** he lived here this morning!

Poor Bear.

He is wet and tired and full, and now his house is
the wrong size too!

He squeezes and wriggles but it's no good. He just
won't fit in.

"I'm stuck!" he cries.

He really is a sad bear.

But who's this coming through
the forest?

"Hello, Bear!" call his friends.
"We've come to thank you."

"You dug up all these carrots,"
says Rabbit.

"And bumped the trees to make the
acorns fall," says Squirrel.

"And you caught all the fish in the river!"
says Beaver.

Bear waves his legs in reply. He feels a little silly
as his friends have to chat to his bottom.

"Now let us help you!" says Rabbit kindly.

They heave and
push until . . .

POP!

Bear is in! It is the right house after all!
  "Thank you, everyone," smiles Bear sleepily.
"Did I really help all of you even though I ate
your food?"

"You really did," says Beaver.

"And you always eat a lot when it's
time to hibernate!" adds Squirrel.

"Hibernate!" yawns Bear happily.
"That's the important thing I have
to remember . . . to . . . do."

Goodnight, Bear.
See you in the spring!

Bear's list of
things to
do today.
1. Eat
2. Sleep

Try these deliciously good reads from Little Tiger!

BUG BEAR

Patricia Hegarty
Carmen Saldaña

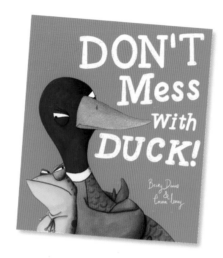

DON'T Mess With DUCK!

Becky Davies & Emma Levey

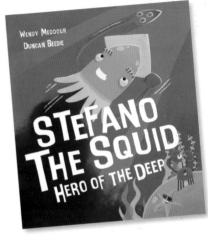

WENDY MEDDOUR
DUNCAN BEEDIE

STEFANO THE SQUID
HERO OF THE DEEP

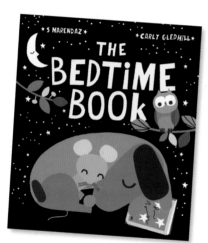

S MARENDAZ   CARLY GLEDHILL

THE BEDTIME BOOK

MEET THE GRUMBLIES

JOHN KELLY   CARMEN SALDAÑA

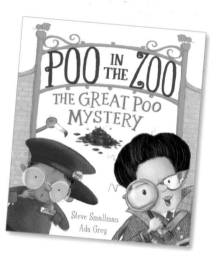

POO IN THE ZOO
THE GREAT POO MYSTERY

Steve Smallman
Ada Grey

LITTLE TIGER

For information regarding any of the above titles or for our catalogue, please contact us: Little Tiger Press Ltd, 1 Coda Studios, 189 Munster Road, London SW6 6AW
Tel: 020 7385 6333 • E-mail: contact@littletiger.co.uk
www.littletiger.co.uk